D0866642

NORTHAMPTON COMMUNITY
DISCARDED

No Heaven

By David St. John

Hush (1976)
The Shore (1980)
No Heaven (1985)

LIMITED EDITIONS:

For Lerida
The Olive Grove
A Folio of Lost Worlds
The Man in the Yellow Gloves

DAVID ST. JOHN

NO HEAVEN

Houghton Mifflin Company · Boston

1985

Library of Congress Cataloging in Publication Data

St. John, David, date
No heaven.

I. Title.
PS3569.A4536N6 1985 811'.54 84-25179
ISBN 0-395-36572-4
ISBN 0-395-36573-2 (pbk.)

Printed in the United States of America

Q 10 9 8 7 6 5 4 3 2 1

The poems in this collection first appeared in the following magazines: *American Poetry Review:* "Two Sorrows"; "A Hard & Noble Patience"; "Wavelength"; "Black Poppy (At the Temple)"; "A Temporary Situation." *Antaeus:* "The Day of the Sentry" copyright © 1984; "The Man in the Yellow Gloves" copyright © 1982. *Crazy Horse:* "The Lemons"; "Meridian." *Field:* "Crossroads." *Grand Street:* "Chapter Forever." *The Iowa Review:* "Winter Fires." *The New Republic:* "Occasions for Monuments." *The New Yorker:* "Desire"; "Shadow"; "The Reef"; "The Swan at Sheffield Park"; "Leap of Faith." *Partisan Review:* "An Essay on Liberation." *Poetry:* "Woman and Leopard"; "No Heaven." *The Yale Review,* copyright Yale University: "Many Rivers"; "The Flute." "The Man in the Yellow Gloves" was also published as a limited edition book by the Penumbra Press.

"The Swan at Sheffield Park" is for Holly and Michael; "The Man in the Yellow Gloves" is for Dan.

I would like to thank the Ingram Merrill Foundation, the Maryland Arts Council, and the National Endowment for the Arts for grants which aided in the completion of this book.

for Norman and Larry
for Julie

CONTENTS

Winter Fires 1
The Day of the Sentry 2
Two Sorrows 4
A Hard & Noble Patience 5
The Lemons 6
Woman and Leopard 8
Many Rivers 12
Desire 13
Shadow 14
Meridian 15
Interlude: Hephaestion's Prayer 17
The Flute 18
Wavelength 20
The Reef 21
The Swan at Sheffield Park 22
Occasions for Monuments 28
Black Poppy (At the Temple) 30
Crossroads 32
Chapter Forever 34
A Temporary Situation 35
Interlude: A Text for Morning 38
An Essay on Liberation 41
The Man in the Yellow Gloves 42
Leap of Faith 50
No Heaven 51

No Heaven

WINTER FIRES

There are lights soft as milk striking
Across the large distant delay
The mistakes the mission the act are all
One with the evening
                                        If any *furthermore*
Still resides in the memory of reeds
Fired beneath the stoked dead limbs of pine
It is only the simple word of it
That future you gave

I will not remain in the remote grain
Of shadow rubbed over
The backdrop of rain *for miles* the rain
Neither will I go forgetting you never
Never even like the cold

I will stand like a flame in the flame

When the frost sears the brass of
The staircase
                        when the heart of shale
Ticks away in the tall cedar clock
Flecks & seconds passing   *passing*
I will stand very still in your absence

Where the shape of the shame has been named

THE DAY OF THE SENTRY

Misery etcetera
Likely as the quilt of leaves
Above this confused congruence of
Sentience

If there were only one path leading away

From the small iron shed
Beside the glass summerhouse where
She sleeps like the broken string of a lute
Like the last in a series of broken
Strings

I might follow that path to the edge
Of the white lake the radical lake rising
All by itself into the air

Where a single cloud descended like a hand

Once while we sat watching
As the moon paced the hard horizon like a sentry
Whose borders had only recently begun
To assemble
Whose latitudes resemble a doubled thread
Whose path remains a sentence on the sleepy tongue

& in that mist of intersection
Lake cloud & moon combining in the slash
Of the instant

I had only the physical to remember you by

Only the heat of your breath along my shoulder
Only the lit web of wet hair streaking
Our faces like the veins of
No other night

No other
Now in the regrettable glare of the mind

Which worships our impermanence
The way in which you have become the *she* asleep
In the summerhouse
where the glass walls
Hold only the gold of the day's light

As if you never had any body I knew at all

TWO SORROWS

He had lived for the sorrow of numbers
& this had made his mind beautiful
& also pure
                    somewhat
Like a globe of red ink held up
In a beaker before the light of the setting
Sun by a woman in a white smock who
Without question desires him
If there is any

Equation he cannot yet complete

It may be that of red ink $\neq$ blood
Though it may also concern the ellipsis of
Sweat along her lips

Beading a bit like the light in the beaker

As he puts his hand around hers for only
A moment & the liquid swirls a little
In the bottom of its glass bulb
& he awakens quite suddenly beyond his dream
Of riverbeds erased by snow
An ostrich at her egg
A boy asleep in the high heavenly forest

Of innumerable & open arms

A HARD & NOBLE PATIENCE

There is a hard & noble patience
I admire in my friends who are dead
Though I admit there are none of them
I would change places with

For one thing look how poorly they dress

Only one is still beautiful
& that is because
She chose to drown herself in a Swiss lake
Fed by a glacier said in local myth
To be a pool of the gods

& when her body was found she was so
Preserved by the icy currents
That even her eyelashes seemed to quiver
Beneath my breath

Though that was only for an instant

Before she was strapped to a canvas stretcher
& loaded into a blue van
Soon I was the only person still standing
At the lake's edge   A man made lonely
By such beauty

A man with less than perfect faith in any god

THE LEMONS

The white villa sat at the lip of rock
Like a slab of ice above the jade
Water & from the village
Across the harbor it seemed to ripple
In the waves of heat rising off the day

He was asleep in the wicker chaise
He'd pulled to the far edge
Of the stone veranda
Dressed in nothing except a black bikini
Suntan oils & a gold link chain
Around his wrist

Unconsciously with one hand he was cupping
His genitals & with the other in his
Sleep swatting flies

She put down the white coffee cup
& walked into the bedroom
Taking from the bottom drawer of the oak
Dresser the small black Beretta
Then she stepped out onto the terrace
Facing away from the sea where the lemon trees
Rose on the near hillside & took aim
At a sequence of possibilities

& on the veranda above the sea
He awoke to the irregular popping of the gun
Echoing through the rooms of the villa
& as he stood up unsteadily
Blinking for a moment in the white glare
He glanced up at the sky & knew
That soon he would be hearing the symphony
Of pans as the cook began the late-afternoon meal

Of rancor & fried eels

WOMAN AND LEOPARD

Jardin des Plantes; the zoo.

Although she was beautiful,
Although her black hair, clipped
Just at the shoulders, glistened
Like obsidian as she moved
With that same slow combination
Of muscles as a dancer stepping
Casually beyond the spotlight
Into the staged, smoky
Blue of the shadows, it was
None of this that bothered me,
That made me follow her as she
Walked with her friends — a couple
Her age — along the wide dirt path
Leading to the island, the circle
Of cages where the cats glared
And paced. She was wearing a leather
Jacket, a simple jacket, cut narrowly
At the waist and dyed a green
I'd always coveted both in
Nature and out. It was the green of
Decay, of earth, of bronze covered by
The fine silt of the city, the green
Of mulch, of vines at the point
Of the most remote depth
In one of Rousseau's familiar jungles;
It was that jacket I was following —
Its epaulets were torn at the shoulders;

The back was crossed by swatches
Of paler, worn horizons
Rubbed away by the backs of chairs;
Along the arms, the scars of cigarettes
And knives, barbed wire . . .
I think it was she who nailed that poster
To the wall of my small room in
The Hôtel des Écoles, an ancient photo
Of the Communards marching in a phalanx
Toward the photographer, tools
And sticks the poor
Weapons held ready in their hands.
It was a poster left up by every
Student or transient spending a night
Or week in that for-real garret,
Its one window opening out
Onto the roof, letting in both
The sunlight and winter rains, the drops
Or streams from the laundry hung to dry
At the window ledge, all of it
Running down along the poster, leaving
Streaks as ocher as the rivers crossing
The map of Europe pinned to the opposite
Wall. On the poster, faded by
Every year, those at the edge of the march
Had grown more and more ghostly, slowly
Evaporating into the sepia; half men,

Half women, half shadow. And I think
It was she in that leather jacket closing
The door to this room in May 1968 to march
With all the other students to the Renault
Factory, to plead again for some
Last unity. Those scars along the arms
Were neatly sutured in that heavy
Coarse thread that sailors use, a thread
Of the same fecund green. The woman,
Thirty-five perhaps, no more, glanced
At me; I watched
As she moved off away from her friends,
Over to the waist-high, horizontal
Steel rail at the front of the leopard's
Cage. I moved to one side, to see both
Her face and the face
Of the leopard she'd chosen to watch;
She began to lock it into her precise,
Cool stare. The leopard sat on
A pillar of rock
Standing between the high metal walkway
At the rear of the cage, where its mate
Strolled lackadaisically, and — below
The leopard — a small pond that stretched
Almost to the cage's front, a pool
Striped blue-and-black by the thin shadows
Of the bars. The woman stood

Very quietly, leaning forward against
The cold steel of the restraint, the rail
Pressing against the bones
Of her hips,
Her hands balled in the pockets
Of her jacket. She kept her eyes on the eyes
Of the leopard . . . ignoring the chatter of
Her friends, of the monkeys, of the macaws.
She cared just for the leopard,
The leopard tensing and arching his back
As each fork of bone pushed up
Along its spine — just
For the leopard
Working its claws along its high perch
Of stone, its liquid jade eyes
Dilating, flashing only for an instant
As the woman suddenly laughed,
And it leapt.

MANY RIVERS

I speak to you like many rivers
Emptying from the heart

This is I know unattractive in a man
Yet when I speak to you in a dialect like wire

Those uneasy words meant to weaken the knees
You will know there's nothing left to abstract

That's not like an idea both vague & elemental
As in say the idea of us which is so

Like the conjugation of rivers
Simply at the heart of the matter

Of these beds of stone & shale giving up giving
Way to every senseless & untimely current

Of the wild convicted flesh

DESIRE

There is a small wrought-iron balcony . . .
& at that balcony she stood a moment
Watching a summer fog
Swirl off the river in huge
Drifting pockets as the street lights grew
Alternately muted then wild then to a blurred
Relay of yellow

Her hair was so blond that from a distance
It shone white as spun silk
& as he turned the corner he stopped suddenly
Looking up at the window of the hotel room
Where she stood in her Japanese kimono
Printed with red dragonflies
& a simple bridge

& in that lapse of breath
As the fog both offered & erased her in the night
He could remember every pulse of her tongue
Every pared detail of constancy left
Only to them   as he began
Walking slowly toward the door of the hotel
Carrying the hard loaf of day-old bread
& plums wrapped in newspaper

Already remembering this past he would desire

SHADOW

I am the shadow you once blessed

Though I was told later you meant only
To bless a small monkey carved of ebony
On the leg of a particular chair

Didn't you notice
That when you fell to your knees I too
Fell & kissed this scarlet earth

Blackened by the lyre of your wings

MERIDIAN

The day seemed suddenly to give to black-&-white
The falcon tearing at the glove
Clare yanking down the hood over its banked eyes
& handing the bird
Its body still rippling & shuddering & flecked
Here or there with blood
                                        to her son Louis
& as we walked back up the overgrown stone trail
To the castle now in the public trust
For tax reasons she admitted
Supposing one more turn in the grave couldn't harm
Her father the Count much at this point anyway
Though she flew his favorite red flag
From one of the towers every year
To mark each anniversary of his death
& though her beauty had acquired the sunken
Sheen of a ship's figurehead lifted
From the clear Mediterranean
As she walked ahead of me in her high chocolate boots
I could think only of her body still muscled like a
Snake's & how she lay sprawled last night
Naked on the blue tiles of the bathroom floor
& as I stepped into the doorway
I could see the bathtub speckled with vomit
The syringe still hanging limply from a vein in her
Thigh & she was swearing

As she grasped for the glass vial
That had rolled out of reach behind the toilet
Then she had it
Drawing herself up slowly as she
Turned her body slightly to look up at me
& she said nothing
Simply waiting until I turned & walked away
The door closing with its soft collapse
Behind me
                    now over lunch on the terrace
I pin a small sprig of parsley to her jacket lapel
A kind of truce   a soldier's decoration
& above us the sun drags the day toward its meridian
Of heat & red wine & circumstance from which
We can neither look back nor step ever
Visibly beyond yet as we
Look at each other in the brash eclipsing glare
We know what bridging silence to respect
Now that neither of us has the heart to care

INTERLUDE: HEPHAESTION'S PRAYER

Because I love you more than any

Forgive me now for leaving you
But please understand how tired I am
This evening
how thirsty & how cold

& though I know it is only the fever
I still wish in my nightmares

I was simply the wind

Then I could speak to you forever after
Whenever the black leaves shook

Because I love you more than any
Please understand I will be as lonely
In whatever place the fever or
The gods will take me

& even if it is not home

Please swear to me
Because you love me more than any

You will not try to follow

THE FLUTE

He'd thrown his wool poncho down onto the packed
Dirt floor of the tool & feed shed
Behind the combination wagon stop & tavern
Where the bartender had led him
With indifferent ceremony speaking the whole
Time in a Spanish that sprayed out incomprehensibly
Through the few remaining stumps of the old man's
Black teeth

Out of a rucksack so limp & worn it resembled
A rotted gourd he took his flute
A long wood flute of local design given to him
By a woman he'd once walked with through
The outskirts of La Paz
While he tested his few phrases against the cage
Of her laughter

Until at last she handed him the flute

As if she meant to show him
Anything he might say to her would grow
Less awkward if spoken with the flute
Which had a voice she already
Desired & understood

The flute he now begins to play
Sitting in the doorway of the decrepit shed

Watching the sullen exhalation of notes
Score a random ladder into the stars
& in spite of the altitude

& in spite of the cold

He continues for hours
Perfecting elaborate variations to the song
Until the old bartender leans out from his upstairs
Window & yells down to him in the name of Christos
Stop for emphasis throwing down into the dirt
A heavy book

Which lands open & on its spine before the doorway
Its pages beginning to turn very slowly for no
Apparent reason & in no wind
As each describes

The silence which has given back the night

WAVELENGTH

They were sitting on the thin mattress
He'd once rolled & carried up the four floors
To his room only to find it covered nearly all
Of the bare wood
Leaving just a small path alongside the wall

& between them was the sack
Of oranges & pears she'd brought its neck
Turned back to expose the colors of the fruit
& as she opened a bottle of wine
He reached over to a tall stack of books
& pulled out *The Tao* & with a silly flourish
Handed it across the bed to her   she looked up
& simply poured the two squat water glasses
Half-full with wine & then she
Took the book   reading silently   not aloud
As he'd assumed & suddenly he felt clearly
She knew the way
Two people must come upon such an understanding
Together of course but separately
As the moon & the wave remain individually one

THE REEF

The most graceful of misunderstandings
I could not keep close at hand
She paused a moment
At the door as she adjusted her scarf against
The winds & sprays & in the moonlight
She rowed back across the inlet to the shore

I sat alone above my pale vodka
Watching its smoky trails of peppercorns
Rising toward my lips

& while I flicked the radio dial
Trying to pick up the Cuban station or even
The static of "The Reggae Rooster" from Jamaica

I watched the waves foam above the coral & recede

Then foam breathlessly again & again
As a school of yellowtail
Rose together to the surface & then suddenly dove
Touched I knew by the long silver glove

Of the barracuda she loved to watch each afternoon
As she let the boat drift in its endlessly

Widening & broken arc

THE SWAN AT SHEFFIELD PARK

It is a dim April
Though perhaps no dimmer than any
London April my friend says
As we turn our backs
To the crooked Thames to the stark
London skyline
                    walking up the hill's
Mild slope to one of the paths
And prospects of Kew
He introduces
The various and gathered families
Of trees then every subtle
Shift of design along the grounds
The carefully laid views and pools
The chapel-sized orangery
Where citrus in their huge trolley tubs
Were wheeled behind the glass walls
And spared each winter
Fresh lime grapefruit and orange
That's what a queen wants
That's what the orangery says
Now April's skies grow a little
More forgiving
Breaking into these tall columns
Of white clouds
                    the kinds of elaborate
Shapes that children call God's Swans

Here in the country an hour
South of London
where Gibbon finished
Decline and Fall in Lord Sheffield's library
In the manor house I can see just there
In the trees
as I walk with my friend along
The road that passes by his cottage
At the edge of the grounds of Sheffield Park
Once again
the sky's high pillars collect
Into one flat unrelieved blanket
Above these shivering leaves
And bent blades
a curtaining mist
Materializes out of the air
As we stop for a moment
On a stone bridge over the small falls
Between two of the lakes
And from the center of one of the lakes
A single swan glides toward us
Its wake a perfect spreading V
Widening along the water
as each arm
Of the V begins to break against
The lake's shores
the swan holds its head

And neck in a classical question mark
The crook of an old man's
Walking stick its eyes fixed on us
As it spreads its wings
In this exact feathery symmetry
Though it does not fly
                                        simply lifting
Its head until the orange beak
Almost touches the apex of the stone
Arch of the bridge
Waiting for whatever crumbs we might
Have thought to bring
For a swan
                    that now turns from us
Gliding with those same effortless gestures
Away without a glance back over
Its smooth shoulder
                                    the mist
Thickens as the clouds drop lower
And the rain threading the branches and leaves
Grows darker and more dense
Until I can barely see the swan on the water
Moving slowly as smoke through this haze
Covering the surface of the lake
That white smudge sailing
To whatever shelter it can find and as
I look again there's nothing
                                                only

The rain pocking the empty table
Of the lake
so even the swan knows
Better than I to get out of the rain
The way it curled white as breath and rose
To nothing along the wind
tonight
By the wood stove of the cottage
Drinking and talking with my friend
I'll tell him about the two women
I saw last week in Chelsea
One of them wrapped in a jumpsuit of wet
Black plastic
her hair coal
Black greased and twirled into spikes
That fell like fingers onto her shoulders
But more alarming
those lines she'd drawn
Out from her mouth with an eyebrow pencil
Along her pale cheeks the perfect
Curved whiskers of a cat
And the other one
her friend dressed
In white canvas painter's pants white leather
Boots and a cellophane blouse
who'd dyed
Her hair utterly white then teased it

So that it rose
Or fell in the breeze lightly and stiffly
As feathers who'd painted her mouth
The same hard rubbery orange as a swan's
And even to a person of no great humor
Or imagination they were

these two

In the silent path they cut in the air
Along King's Road in every way
Beautiful

and for the rest

Of the day I was so shaken I made
Myself stop for a drink in Soho
A strip joint called *The Blade*
I'd stumbled into and judging from my
Welcome not a place for the delicate
But I stuck it out through enough Scotch
To make me drunk fearless
And screaming through the first show
When at its end the final stripper
Stepped from the small stage right onto the bar top
Everyone clearing away the glasses and bottles
From the polished copper in front of them
As she threw off everything strutting
Down the narrow bar except
A white boa G-string
Shivering against her thighs as she

Kicked her silver high heels to either side
Then lay down in front of me
Her bare back and shoulders pressed flat
To the copper as it steamed and smudged beneath
Her body's heat
the catcalls and hollers
Rising as she lifted each leg
Pointing her toes to the spotlights scattered
Across the ceiling
her legs held in a pale V
The silver sequins of her high heels
Glittering in the lights but
Then she stood abruptly
And stepped back onto the stage not
Waiting a moment before turning her back
To the hoarse cheers
disappearing
In the sheer misty gauze of the old curtains
And as the lights came up there was
Where she'd been
Just the trails and webs of cigarette smoke
Those long curlicues in a tattoo of light
Those ghosts and feathers of dust
Still drifting down onto the bare tables
The glistening bar
onto the empty veiled stage
Of wood warped gently as waves

OCCASIONS FOR MONUMENTS

For once she knew why she loved New England
As she walked that wet afternoon
Through the streets of the small town
Where her father'd been raised
It was the homely eloquence
That found such occasions for monuments
Bronze plaques bolted into old brick
The heroes & heroines planted on their plinths
In each town square & courtyard

Though that morning as she'd listened
To the minister recite her father's virtues
As if they were the simple
Virtues of all mankind native to Massachusetts
She could think only of the sound
The dirt made as
It broke over the black lid of the casket
& she wanted the moment to be somehow
Less polite

She wanted

To be back upstairs in her old room
That he'd kept for her exactly
As she'd asked
Even though he'd once called it in a letter
As a joke *St. Joan's immaculate cell*

& as she sat at her desk with its view
Of the square & the green grid of lawn & path

She smoothed with one hand the rippled felt
Of the tobacco-colored writing pad
Covering the desk's mahogany
& placed there the two gifts he'd once
Brought her
                    a glass pyramid from Venice
Its peak opaque as frost but clearing
To a base of the palest blue
& beside it the tooled ivory figure
Of a monk carved with the patience of a monk

& as the light faded at dusk
She looked out at the statues & memorials
So resolutely gray beneath a graying sky

Then glanced down
At the monk & pyramid lit by the brass desk lamp
Where they stood upon the worn browns of
The soft felt landscape   glowing   each so
White & luminous against the gaining dark

Pulsing in unnatural relief

BLACK POPPY (AT THE TEMPLE)

Perhaps it's a question of what
The ruins will accept   a simple flower
Or a few casual hymns by the side
Of this narrow mountain road
Where the dusty cones of sunlight are falling
Through the afternoon air
& the marble ribs of the temple are starting to blur
As the tourists come back across the fields

He slid down off the dented hood of the car
To open the door for them & acknowledge
Their praise of the view

Yet as he glanced out of habit into the side mirror
The hammered whiteness of his own face
Startled him & on
The drive back down the steep cobbled road
To the hotel in the valley   he knew that it was

Time he left his closet not a room at the rear
Of the hotel filled it seemed
With nothing but dull paintings & moldering books
& maps no one unfolded
                                        time to walk away
From all of the habits that owned him especially
The habit of dreams

& that evening as he drove back up the road
Toward the crest of stars above the temple
Those ruins where he could walk & pray
To nothing

He knew that in every one of those dreams
He'd always be a dead man   just a suicide of
Elegant but precise intent
Dressed in a white summer suit & wearing
On his lapel an exquisite & dramatic black poppy

A hand-stitched blossom of glazed silk
Black as the shadow of a real poppy   black as
That moist bud of opium

Pinned to no memory of a living man

CROSSROADS

It was the privilege of the wind
To leave without apology

Of the moon to purse serenely in the sky

As she came to the crossroads
Where the one main road for miles met
The lane from the church
She looked up at the two pre-Revolutionary
Houses standing one to either side
Of the far arm of the cross
Where the main road mounted a hill & disappeared

The stone house was set back into a crescent
Of high gravemarkers & old maples
& in the yellow frame house across from it
She could see by its lit windows the young man
& younger woman who'd recently moved in
& what sort of people she wondered
Could paint a house yellow as an oilslicker

Lighting a cigarette she looked beyond
The slope of the fields
To the cresting shoulders of the white mountains
& the few peaks sparking in the erratic
Touch-&-go of autumn moonlight

Hesitating at the crossroads
She turned & began walking down the church lane
To give herself a few more minutes before
Returning home
                              pleased & astonished
That between striking the match & lifting it
To her cigarette she'd decided once & for all

Again she'd never leave him

CHAPTER FOREVER

I remember I was 9 or 10   so the year I guess
Was 1959   my aunt was showing me the city
Of Sausalito   & the houseboats
Where some of her friends had once lived

On a patch of grass by the sidewalk
A girl sat with her legs crossed   holding
In her left hand a perfectly blank tablet
The size of a transistor radio   & in her right
An unused pen   she was staring right out
Into the Pacific   & as we walked by
My aunt shrugged & said   *Too bad   No inspiration*

We passed a coffee shop
& in its doorway a couple stood just talking
He was on the top step & she was looking up at him
From the step below   he rubbed his beard   & as
We passed he winked at us   *That's Lenny Bruce*
My aunt said quietly & though we kept on walking
After a block or so   I turned around to see

He was still joking with the woman
Palms upturned he was slowly drawing both arms up
Into a full cross   his head fell limply to one side
& the woman started laughing even harder   I remember
She was laughing so hard pretty soon she was almost
Bent over   almost crying   I think   crying

A TEMPORARY SITUATION

Once I was in love with a woman
& though it was a temporary situation
By that I mean an affair of only
A few weeks   still it's true
I was so in love I was really quite
Out of my mind I mean truly mad

& this woman had led   well
A very difficult & complicated life
On several continents with what seemed
To have been countless lovers
Though once in fact I did try counting
& lost track almost immediately

Once in a while at dinner
Suddenly whole years would shift away
& she'd be talking to people
Who simply weren't there
People I knew she'd once loved & spent
Hours with daily but who without question
Were no longer there

So I found my madness was nothing
Held up next to hers though I'd wanted
To make our madness one

& the entire time we were together

I swear to you it was every night
Sometimes at 2 or 3 A.M.
Though most often just before sunrise
She'd sit bolt upright in bed   staring

Off into the distance somewhere beyond the wall

At some figure or horizon she could never quite
Speak of

Though her eyes were enormous with her terror
& still she just sat there trembling
As the sweat
Rolled off her shoulders & along her breasts
Which rocked slightly as she shook

I'd put my arms around her as she awakened
Slowly into the morning
Telling her over & over again first the name
Of the city in which she was living

& then my own name

Several times   I'd have to tell her my own name
Because you see at those times she'd have
Forgotten everything & I was part
Of that   I mean everything

She could no longer recognize
When she awoke on the other side of the world

Where   I believe   nothing is taken for granted

INTERLUDE: A TEXT FOR MORNING

Time is a performance   staged daily   yet
Necessarily repetitious   a day returns preceded by
a slur of fortune   a silver light edged
With white-throated sparrows & the fur of blown
summer weeds   even as the least fortunate
Of chimes recurs   we listen   nevertheless
for what the silence opposes   minus
A fissure in time   as if one of the terms of
the metaphor had left disguised   equally
Our kinship to the oblique   the whole scrim slowly
shaking   yet I can see   a body   yours
& the black geese across the morning occur like
delicate sutures in the sky   connecting
What is not us   & beyond   until even the form (of
light) frames the subjective   image is light
In space   or its absence   I mean   the dark of
space between bodies   the way   every story
Suffers this construction of figure   in time   as
every episode announces its private system of
Blows & fragments   so please   leave me alone with
my ideologies   my one ghostly significance
Nailed against the facts   you were   when the history
of light is again rewritten   include me here
At the lip of nothing   that is   the day   oh look at
the fields you might say   the fields are so close
But the fields are moving   in the light   so tell me
which are the fields   where is the light

Or were you only pointing to those fields of light
above the other fields   those repetitions of
The gold veneer of bodies by the fire   fire of bodies
rising with the sun   one & the other   one
These are the questions no one assumes   to begin so
easily in light   existing   first
In negative   (image)   black-&-white   footnotes
to memory   those astonished wounds in the elision
Of field   (light/lost)   & does every image
stitch itself to song   does the "real" desire its
Emblem in the mind   will the hero find his beloved
in the first reel   or the last   when the cinema
Empties & the sky acquires its intricate code of stars
what will have been their future   the geometry
They trusted in descent   across a circumstance
advertised as "real"   & finally   as the glass curtains
Are drawn in the bedroom   & the frame of the moment
is held   the phasing of phrases   the slow
Tableau of fucking   that truculent lucency of bodies
in the dark   the fiction falls   & only the economy of
Night is left   walking the last corridor   I sense
your body   (the dark)   (the light)   so
I choose the interval between   that is   you   still
tiny eclipses   flashes of chains   after all
This is simply a kind of wailing   (nothing)   a keening
for a body in the dark   a lost body   yet
In the margins of the day   you remain   curled & precise

as the serifs in a latticework of brown ink slowly
Coiling down the page   the light glossing the fields
just as I'm about to turn away   & the hills ride out
To the sea   (under the sun)   & I'm alone with
lilies in my hand   at this empty foyer in the pines
Where no one waits   & this is   naturally
the condition of illusion   the way   the body
Is to be the predicate of light   the dark screen now
filling suddenly with the silver scrub of day
Memory   recovery   history   all struggling with the text
even after the mourning subsides   question:
What was the way before the destination (first) existed
the way was: you   & a passionate light
Dissolves the horizon   washing the hung double moon
& in that light   I'll be left only the holy past
Its useless snapshots   its cancelled letters
its one figure hovering against the cold ground
So the stage is cleared again of the lovely incidentals
which make us believe we wish to live   &
Like the shadow of a statue at dawn   I am yours
& yet am not you   the voice I am is again
The silence between steps   as you pass before a window
damp with ash   still lit by the night's mirror

AN ESSAY ON LIBERATION

He stood naked at one of the two windows
She kept open in all weathers   in her
Corner room at the back of the old building
As the sun rose   he watched a man
Dragging a handcart along the narrow alley below
& across the court a young boy was turning
His face from side to side in a freckled mirror
From the temples in the old section of the city
He could hear the first sequence
Of morning prayers   & to the west he could see
The dulled bronze domes of The Church of the Orthodox
Where at any moment the bells would begin to chime
& in the streets crisscrossing the city
From the old section to the sea
The tanks & personnel trucks began moving quietly
Into position in their orderly & routine way
& as the bells began sounding from their tower
They were answered by the echoing concussion of mortars
As the daily shelling of the hills began
& she was slicing small pieces of bread the size of coins
To fry in goat butter & chives   she was naked
Kneeling on one of the worn rugs thrown at angles across
The scarred floor   she glanced up at him & smiled
Nodding for no reason in particular   & in spite of
The fact the one phrase he'd taught her perfectly
Began with the word for *free*   though it ended
With *nothing*

THE MAN IN THE YELLOW GLOVES

"They were kept in a wooden trunk
In one corner of the attic
A trunk my grandfather had painted
With red and black enamels
In the manner of the Chinese cabinets
He loved and could not afford
And inside the trunk the small box
Lined with a violet velvet
Where he kept his gloves
                                        a box
That I believe should have held
A strand of pearls or a set
Of bone-handled
Carving knives from Geneva
A box fluted with ivory
And engraved with my grandfather's
Initials each letter
Still faintly visible in its flourish
Of script across the tiny brass shield
Holding the latch
                              one night
My mother dragged it out to remind
Herself of a particular
Summer at the lake when her father
Dressed to the teeth for once
In his life arrived at
The lake shore for a cocktail party

At a neighbor's boat and stepped
Right off into the water
Trying to stretch the short distance
From the dock to the boat's deck
And though the water was extremely shallow
All anyone could see for a moment
Were his hands held barely
Up in the twilight up
Above the surface of the water
Not pleading for help not reaching for
A rope but simply keeping his gloves
Dry his gloves of lemon silk
Which he refused to let touch water
Or liquid of any kind but
He rose slowly in the foam
Walking up the muddy rocks kicking
And swearing
Making his way over to the lake's edge
His hands still held up as if
At gunpoint
To the applause of the whole
Party my mother said as she worked
The frozen clasp loose of its pin
And slid her fingernail along
The edges of the box
Where the mold held it
Until the thin lid peeled back

And inside
                    the yellow silk
Lit against the violet lining
Each finger of each glove bent
Slightly in an undisturbed
Calm
The two thumbs folded
Precisely across the palms
As if to guard the long seams
Crossing each like a lifeline
And my mother held the two gloves
Up to the light to let us see
Their transparence
                                        a glow
Like the wings of a flying fish
As it clears the sea's surface
Then she laid them in my own
Cupped hands
Each as faintly moist as a breath
And as she smoothed them again
Along the velvet of their box
I imagined how I might someday pull
Them on in elegant company
Though even then the gloves were as small
As my hands
And so the next summer with my family
Camping near that familiar lake

I decided one night to find the old dock
Long since replaced by a new marina
I took the kerosene lamp
And walked to the main road
Then along its low curving shoulders
Until I came to the pitted asphalt lane
That once led to the dock
I picked my way slowly through the rubble
Through the brush and overgrown branches
The small globe of light thrown
By the lamp falling
Ahead of me along the path
Until I could see the brief glitter
And glare of the lake
Where the stars had escaped their clouds
And stood reflected

and where the road

Once swung gently toward the pier
The rocks now fell off 20 feet
In a sudden shelf and at its bottom
The dark planking of the dock began
I held the lamp in both hands
Pressing my back against
The slick dirt-and-stone face of the shelf
I slid carefully down working the heels
Of my boots into the crags and juts
To slow myself in the clatter

Of twigs and gravel old
Paving rotted boards and bark
Until I stopped and caught my breath
Looking out over the old dock
The soft planks at my feet stretching
Past the water's edge
Held up still by a few fat pilings
And as I took the first
Of a few steps
                    the moldered boards
Sagged and snapped beneath me splinters
Shooting up as I tried to leap clear
As one ankle twisted in the broken planks
And I fell face down onto the mossy
Dock the lamp
I'd been holding the whole time
Smashing in my hands the kerosene
Washing over the boards and my fingers
Up past both wrists and blazing
In a sudden and brilliant gasp of flame
I held up my burning hands
Yanking my leg up through the shattered boards
Rolling then falling onto the rocks below
My hands still aflame each a flat
Candle boned with five wicks
And then I remember only
The hospital in the village

Then the hospital in the city where
I lay for weeks
My hands bandaged and rebandaged
Like heavy wooden spoons
And beneath the crisp daily
Gauze the skin of each hand was seared
And blistered each finger raw
The pores dilating as the burnt skin
Was first bared to the air then to
The ointments
And each day more morphine
As the fever rose up my arms into
My mind my dreams until the morphine
Dimmed the nights and days
Until at last even I could stand to look
At the gnarled and shrunken hands
As if some child had made
The skeletons of wire
Then wrapped each poorly in doughy strings
Of papier-mâché

in the next year

My hands were stitched in a patchwork
Of dime-sized pieces of skin cut
And lifted from the small
Of my back or my legs
Until they began to resemble
Hands you might hold in your own

But since then and in the hottest
Weather it doesn't matter I've
Always worn these gloves
Not from any
Vanity but to spare myself and you
The casual looking away
These gloves of kid leather tanned
Soft as skin and dyed at my request
A pale yellow
                the yellow of a winter lemon
In honor of my grandfather in honor
Of the fire as it dies
And if some men choose to walk
Miles in the country just
To look across the patches and divides
Of the landscape
Into the hills lakes and valleys
Or the dense levels of tree and cloud
So that they might better meditate upon
Their world their bitterness fatigue
Themselves well
I have only to take off one glove
Or another to stare down into the landscape
Of each scorched stitched hand
At the melted webs of flesh at the base
Of each finger
                the depressions

Or small mounts and lumps of scar
The barely covered bone
or the palms
Burnt clean of any future any
Mystery so I'll pull back on
My gloves these
That I order each year from London
And if in the course of a dinner somewhere
I hear comments about the arrogance
Of a man who'd wear his gloves
Through an entire meal what a dandy
What an out-of-date mannered sort of parody
Of a gentleman
I will not mind
If the mild shock and disapproval rise
When I wear my yellow gloves
I'll never pull one off to startle
Or shame everyone into silence
instead
I'll simply check to see that each glove
Is properly secure
that each pearl button
Is snugly choked in its taut loop
Its minute noose of leather"

LEAP OF FAITH

No less fabulous than the carved marble inner
Ear of a lost Michelangelo & more
Blinding than the multiple courts & interior facets
Of a black diamond held up in broken moonlight

This final geography acknowledges its trunks of
Ebony & its boughs of summer rain

Though there at the gate where Dante burned his
Initials into the face of the oak shield
I hesitated before following the switchback trail up
To the precipice overlooking the canyon the abyss
So relished by philosophy & when I saw you
On the opposite cliff in your long cape & gold
Shoes with frayed thin ribbons snaking up your ankles

Like anyone approaching from the foot of a bridge
I simply stepped toward you & below the bones
Of the fallen shone in the lightning & the prayers

& certainly it was there in that country
Braced between twin brackets of stone I saw only one
Belief remains for a man whose life is spared by

A faith more insupportable than air

NO HEAVEN

This is the last prayer in the book
Of black prayers   a last
Passionate *yes*

Against bad timing & bad luck

& what else
Could be delivered beyond request
Except: *the living & the dead*

So I'll lay these carved shadow-figures

To rest along the rough rack pallet
Beneath the bed   though
Their shadows still continue   poor pilgrims

Walking the curved white stucco arch
Above our heads   & after
You wake to the scraping of these pine limbs
Against the unlatched windowpane

I'll smooth the delicate line & lace of sweat
That trims your hair's damp open fan
Along the folded pillow

The fever's watermark as it slowly stains
The forehead just as the tides of the canal

Measure these erratic summer rains
Streaking the sheer cement banks & high walls
As the debris of the city

Rises endlessly   & then endlessly falls

& I remember how the light with its simplicity
Frames always the lasting shape
Of your body   (standing)   at the jetty's end

& in the dream: *I'm running toward*

You to drape a silver raincoat   across your
Uncovered shoulders as you turn & the
World flares   & we wait

For an ending that grows irrevocably older
As in every apocalyptic play
& settling on us   upon the jetty   an ash colder

Than   in winter   the iron lattice
Of the cage I grip with both hands as I speak
To the albino mandrill   (at the Historical Zoo)

Not all but some days about the eclipse

Of earth   & flesh   & brick
Though no matter how I've tried   no matter
All of the horrible things I've said

The only response I can ever provoke

Is a few bared teeth as he throws
Back his head   & screams
                                        Is that really
For all of the dead   a child by me
Asked her mother once & then she
Continued   *I mean all of the dead he remembers*
From his monkey dreams

In my dreams the world dies also in white embers

Not ash of course but blown light   drifting
Over the jetty   silently   forever

Yet this morning as I look very
Closely into the dresser mirror I can see
There in my own face

The hard meridian crossed & then re-crossed
  Hope   the new year

& yours is the name I'll say again & again

Until I'm sure this world can't force apart
The simple pulse of heaven
From the elaborate music of the heart

& all I want is for this sickness to have passed

Leaving us the ordinary world
Whole & rising in the dark *this* world *this* earth

& walking calmly toward us out of the broken mists

The figure whose passion remains the single
Gift (yet) who now at last admits
That we're to be given no heaven

No heaven but this